NANA, I WANT TO PRAISE THE LORD!
COLORING BOOK

This Book Belongs To:

_____

Illustrations and Story by Tranise Jenkins

Copyright © 2022 Tranise Jenkins
All Rights Reserved

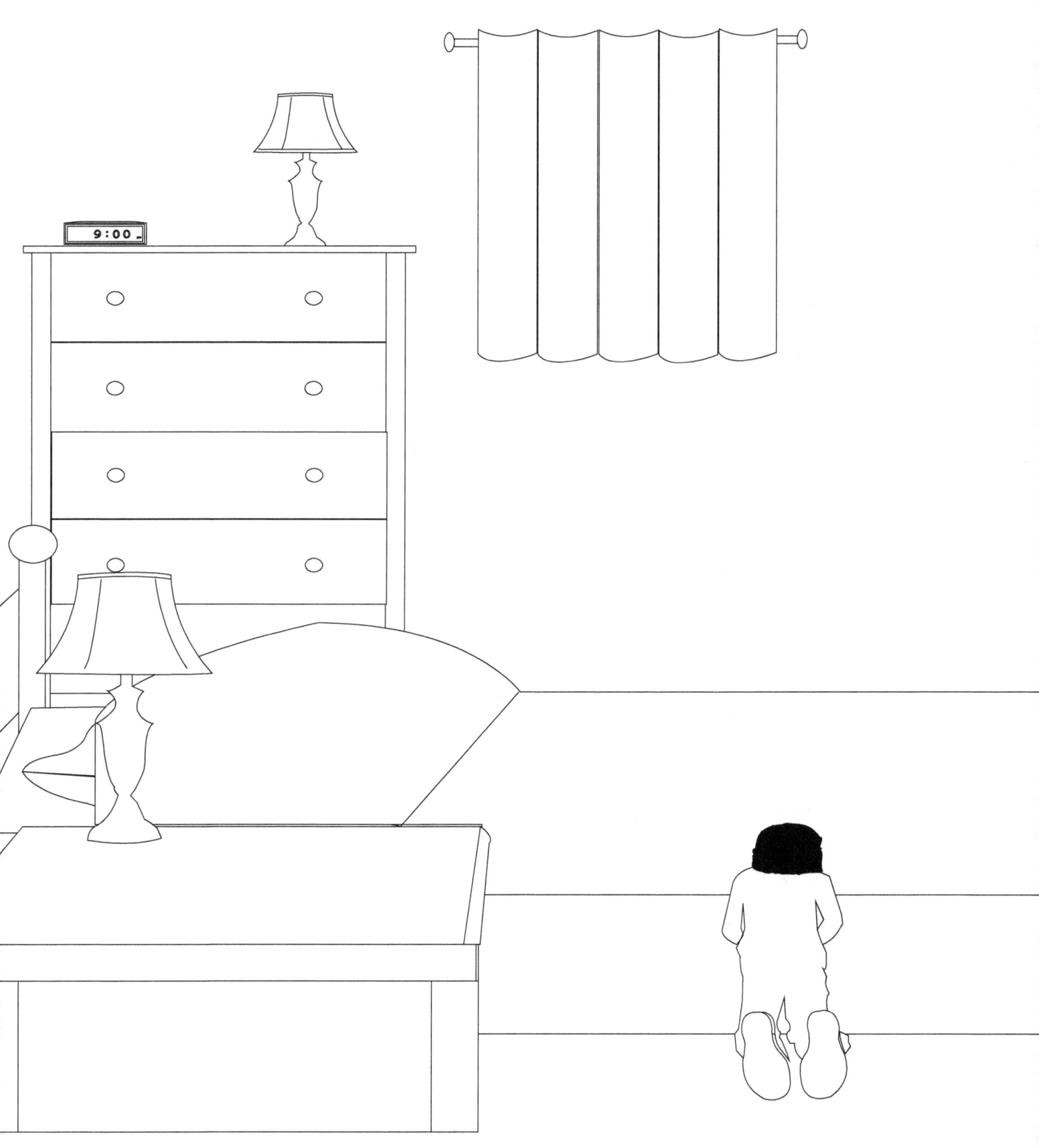

NANA, I WANT TO PRAISE THE LORD

Other Coloring Books by Tranise Jenkins

mybestfriendsnuff.com